GOD'S DNA

Dr. Maxwell Shimba

Published in Manhattan, New York by Shimba Publishing, LLC.

Shimba Publishing, LLC

Printed in the United States of America

First Printing Edition 2024

TABLE OF CONTENTS

Introduction v

PART I 1

DNA 1

Chapter 1 2

Understanding 2

Chapter 02 6

The Biblical Meaning of DNA: Did It Change Your Life? 6

Chapter 03 12

Adamic DNA 12

Chapter 04 18

Master Your Allegiance in God's DNA 18

Chapter 05 24

The DNA of Man: Did It Change Your Life? 24

Chapter 06 30

Discovering Your True Self 30

Chapter 07 35

The Power of Divine Perspective 35

Chapter 08 40

The Quest for Approval 40

Chapter 09 45

The Power of Integrity 45

PART II 50

DNA in the Bible 50

Chapter 10 51

The Divine Blueprint 51

Chapter 11 56

DNA and Human 56

Chapter 12 61
DNA: The Spiritual Dimension 61
Chapter 13 66
Why DNA is Spiritual? 66
Chapter 14 71
Embracing God's DNA 71
Chapter 15 75
The relationship between God's DNA and Human DNA 75
PART III 81
Forensic DNA 81
Chapter 16 82
The Power of DNA in Forensic Science 82
Chapter 17 88
The Spiritual Dimension of DNA in Forensic Science 88
Chapter 18 94
Jesus as the Way and Truth: A Comparison with Forensic Science in Solving Problems 94
Chapter 19 100
Concluding the Book of God's DNA and Its Importance in Understanding God 100

INTRODUCTION

The Relationship Between God's DNA, Adamic DNA, and Forensic Science

Understanding the Connections

In exploring the profound relationship between God's DNA, Adamic DNA, and forensic science, we delve into the realms of theology, biology, and criminal justice. These connections illuminate how our spiritual and physical identities intersect and how modern science can reveal deeper truths about our nature and origins. This chapter examines the interrelatedness of these concepts, providing a comprehensive understanding of their significance.

God's DNA: The Divine Blueprint

God's DNA can be understood as the spiritual essence and divine image imprinted upon humanity. Genesis 1:27 (NIV) states:

"So God created mankind in his own image, in the image of God he created them; male and female he created them."

This passage signifies that humans are created with a divine imprint, reflecting God's attributes such as creativity, moral reasoning, and relational capacity. This divine blueprint forms the foundation of our spiritual identity and purpose.

Adamic DNA: The Human Condition

Adamic DNA refers to the physical and spiritual nature inherited from Adam, the first human according to the Bible. Genesis 2:7 (NIV) describes the creation of Adam:

"Then the LORD God formed a man from the dust of the ground and breathed into his nostrils the breath of life, and the man became a living being."

Adam's DNA represents the initial state of human perfection, imbued with both physical and spiritual vitality. However, the Fall introduced sin and corruption into this DNA. Romans 5:12 (NIV) explains:

"Therefore, just as sin entered the world through one man, and death through sin, and in this way death came to all people because all sinned."

This inherited sinful nature, often referred to as original sin, affects all of humanity, creating a need for redemption and restoration.

Forensic Science: The Search for Truth

Forensic science applies scientific methods to solve crimes and uncover truths. DNA analysis is a cornerstone of forensic science, enabling the identification of individuals and the resolution of criminal cases. This scientific pursuit aligns with the biblical principle of seeking truth. John 8:32 (NIV) states:

"Then you will know the truth, and the truth will set you free."

Forensic science, through the analysis of DNA, reveals hidden truths and brings clarity to complex situations, paralleling the spiritual quest for understanding and justice.

The Interplay of God's DNA and Adamic DNA

The concept of God's DNA and Adamic DNA highlights the dual nature of humanity—created in the divine image yet marred by sin. This interplay is crucial for understanding human identity and destiny. Ephesians 4:22-24 (NIV) instructs:

"You were taught, with regard to your former way of life, to put off your old self, which is being corrupted by its deceitful desires; to be made new in the attitude of your minds; and to put on the new self, created to be like God in true righteousness and holiness."

The transformative power of redemption through Christ offers a way to restore the divine image within us, overcoming the corrupted Adamic DNA.

Forensic Science and the Redemption Narrative

Forensic science, particularly DNA analysis, can be seen as a metaphor for the redemptive work of Christ. Just as forensic scientists analyze DNA to uncover the truth and bring justice, Christ's sacrifice and resurrection provide a way to restore our spiritual DNA. 1 Corinthians 15:21-22 (NIV) states:

"For since death came through a man, the resurrection of the dead comes also through a man. For as in Adam all die, so in Christ all will be made alive."

This parallel emphasizes the transformative power of truth and redemption, both in forensic science and in the spiritual realm.

The Ethical Implications

The intersection of God's DNA, Adamic DNA, and forensic science also raises important ethical considerations. The use of DNA in forensic science must be guided by principles of justice, privacy, and respect for human dignity. Proverbs 2:6-9 (NIV) highlights the importance of wisdom and ethical conduct:

"For the LORD gives wisdom; from his mouth come knowledge and understanding. He holds success in store for the upright, he is a shield to those whose walk is blameless, for he guards the course of the just and protects the way of his faithful ones."

Applying this wisdom ensures that the powerful tools of forensic science are used ethically and justly, honoring the divine image in every individual.

Connecting the Dots: A Unified Perspective

Understanding the connections between God's DNA, Adamic DNA, and forensic science provides a unified perspective on human identity and destiny. These connections highlight the interplay of physical and spiritual realities and the transformative power of truth and redemption. Colossians 1:16-17 (NIV) underscores the coherence of all creation:

"For in him all things were created: things in heaven and on earth, visible and invisible, whether thrones or powers or rulers or authorities; all things have been created through him and for him. He is before all things, and in him all things hold together."

This holistic view affirms that science and spirituality are not mutually exclusive but complementary in revealing the fullness of truth.

Conclusion: Embracing the Fullness of Truth

The relationship between God's DNA, Adamic DNA, and forensic science underscores the profound connections between our spiritual and physical identities. By recognizing these connections, we gain a deeper understanding of our nature, our need for redemption, and the pursuit of truth in all aspects of life.

As we conclude this chapter, let us embrace the fullness of truth revealed through both science and faith. By integrating these perspectives, we honor the divine image within us and commit to living with integrity, justice, and a deeper understanding of our Creator's purpose for our lives. This integrated approach enriches our journey, guiding us to live in alignment with the divine blueprint and the transformative power of redemption.

DR. MAXWELL SHIMBA

PART I

DNA

CHAPTER 1

UNDERSTANDING

What is DNA?

DNA, or deoxyribonucleic acid, is the hereditary material in humans and almost all other organisms. Nearly every cell in a person's body has the same DNA. Most DNA is located in the cell nucleus (where it is called nuclear DNA), but a small amount of DNA can also be found in the mitochondria (where it is called mitochondrial DNA or mtDNA). The information in DNA is stored as a code made up of four chemical bases: adenine (A), guanine (G), cytosine (C), and thymine (T).

These bases pair up with each other, A with T and C with G, to form units called base pairs. Each base pair attaches to a sugar molecule and a phosphate molecule to form a nucleotide. These nucleotides are arranged in two long strands that form a spiral called a double helix. The structure of the double helix is somewhat like a ladder, with the base pairs forming the ladder's rungs and the sugar and phosphate molecules forming the vertical sidepieces of the ladder.

The Role of DNA

DNA contains the instructions needed for an organism to develop, survive, and reproduce. It does this by controlling the production of proteins. Proteins are complex molecules that play many critical roles in the body. They do most of the work in cells and are required for the structure, function, and regulation of the body's tissues and organs.

Each DNA sequence that contains instructions to make a protein is known as a gene. Humans have approximately 20,000 to 25,000 genes. Genes are arranged on chromosomes. In humans, each cell normally contains 23 pairs of chromosomes, for a total of 46. Twenty-two of these pairs, called autosomes, look the same in both males and females. The 23rd pair, the sex chromosomes, differ between males and females.

DNA Replication

One of the most important properties of DNA is its ability to replicate, or make copies of itself. This process is crucial because when cells divide, each new cell needs to have an exact copy of the DNA present in the old cell. The structure of the double helix allows DNA to be copied accurately.

During replication, the two strands of DNA separate. Each strand serves as a template for the creation of a new complementary strand. The result is two DNA molecules, each with one old and one new strand. This process is facilitated by enzymes called DNA polymerases.

Mutations in DNA

Sometimes errors occur during DNA replication. These errors are called mutations. Mutations can be caused by environmental factors such as UV light, chemicals, or viruses, or they can occur naturally. Mutations can lead to changes in the protein produced, which can have various effects on an organism's health and development. While some mutations can be harmful or cause diseases, others can be neutral or even beneficial, leading to evolutionary changes.

Significance of DNA in Medicine

Understanding DNA has revolutionized medicine and biotechnology. Genetic research has led to advancements in diagnosing and treating genetic disorders, developing gene therapies, and personalizing medicine based on individual genetic profiles. The Human Genome Project, completed in 2003, mapped all the genes in the human genome, providing a valuable resource for medical research and the understanding of human biology.

Conclusion

DNA is the fundamental building block of life, carrying the genetic instructions that shape who we are and how we function. Its discovery has transformed our understanding of biology and opened new frontiers in medicine and biotechnology. As we delve deeper into the complexities of DNA, we uncover more about the intricacies of life itself, and as we will explore in the following chapters, the profound connection between our genetic makeup and our spiritual essence.

CHAPTER 02

THE BIBLICAL MEANING OF DNA: DID IT CHANGE YOUR LIFE?

DNA and Divine Design

DNA, the molecule that carries genetic instructions for life, has revolutionized our understanding of biology and medicine. But beyond its scientific implications, DNA can also be viewed through a biblical lens, providing deeper insights into our spiritual identity and purpose. This chapter explores the biblical meaning of DNA and how this understanding can transform our lives.

The Biblical Perspective on Creation

The Bible begins with the account of creation, where God speaks life into existence. Genesis 1:27 (NIV) states:

"So God created mankind in his own image, in the image of God he created them; male and female he created them."

Being created in God's image implies that our very essence is a reflection of the divine. This divine imprint can be likened to our spiritual DNA, which encompasses not only our physical attributes but also our moral and spiritual capacities.

The Divine Blueprint

Psalm 139:13-14 (NIV) beautifully describes the intimate involvement of God in our creation:

"For you created my inmost being; you knit me together in my mother's womb. I praise you because I am fearfully and wonderfully made; your works are wonderful, I know that full well."

This passage emphasizes that our formation is not a random occurrence but a purposeful act of divine craftsmanship. Just as DNA contains the instructions for our physical development, God's Word contains the blueprint for our spiritual growth and purpose.

Spiritual Inheritance and Identity

The concept of inheritance is central to the biblical narrative. Ephesians 1:11 (NIV) explains:

"In him we were also chosen, having been predestined according to the plan of him who works out everything in conformity with the purpose of his will."

This inheritance includes both our spiritual DNA and the promises of God. Understanding our identity as children of God, chosen and predestined for His purposes, provides a foundation for living a life aligned with His will.

The Fall and Redemption

The narrative of Adam and Eve's disobedience in Genesis 3 introduces the concept of sin, which has tainted human nature. Romans 5:12 (NIV) explains:

"Therefore, just as sin entered the world through one man, and death through sin, and in this way death came to all people, because all sinned."

This inherited sin nature, often referred to as the "Adamic nature," affects our spiritual DNA. However, the redemptive work of Jesus Christ offers a path to restoration. 1 Corinthians 15:22 (NIV) declares:

"For as in Adam all die, so in Christ all will be made alive."

Through faith in Christ, we receive a new spiritual identity, characterized by righteousness and eternal life.

Transformation Through Spiritual Rebirth

Jesus speaks of the necessity of spiritual rebirth in John 3:3 (NIV):

"Jesus replied, 'Very truly I tell you, no one can see the kingdom of God unless they are born again.'"

This new birth signifies a transformation of our spiritual DNA, where the old sinful nature is replaced with a new nature aligned with God's will. 2 Corinthians 5:17 (NIV) affirms:

"Therefore, if anyone is in Christ, the new creation has come: The old has gone, the new is here!"

This transformation is the essence of living out our spiritual DNA, reflecting God's character in our lives.

Living According to God's Blueprint

The Bible provides the guidelines for living a life that honors our divine design. Ephesians 4:22-24 (NIV) instructs:

"You were taught, with regard to your former way of life, to put off your old self, which is being corrupted by its deceitful desires; to be made new in the attitude of your minds; and to put on the new self, created to be like God in true righteousness and holiness."

Aligning our lives with God's Word helps us to live out the new spiritual DNA we have received through Christ.

Impact on Personal Life: Did It Change Your Life?

Understanding the biblical meaning of DNA can profoundly impact our lives. Here are a few ways this understanding might change your life:

1. Enhanced Self-Worth: Recognizing that you are "fearfully and wonderfully made" and created in the image of God can enhance your self-worth and confidence. You are valued and cherished by the Creator of the universe.

2. Purpose and Direction: Understanding that you are part of God's divine plan provides a sense of purpose and direction. Your life has meaning and significance beyond earthly achievements.

3. Moral and Spiritual Growth: Embracing your new spiritual DNA in Christ encourages moral and spiritual growth. It calls you to live a life of righteousness, reflecting God's character in your actions and decisions.

4. Resilience and Hope: The promise of redemption and eternal life through Christ gives you resilience in the face of life's challenges and hope for the future. You are part of a larger story of redemption and restoration.

5. Community and Belonging: Knowing that you are part of God's family fosters a sense of community and belonging. You are connected to a global body of believers who share your faith and values.

Conclusion: Embracing Your Divine Design

The biblical meaning of DNA provides a profound understanding of our identity and purpose. By recognizing the divine imprint in our creation, the impact of sin, and the redemptive power of Christ, we can embrace our spiritual DNA and live out God's blueprint for our lives.

As we conclude this chapter, let us reflect on the transformative power of understanding our divine design. By aligning our lives with God's Word and embracing our new identity in Christ, we can experience the fullness of life that God intends for us. This understanding can indeed change our lives, providing clarity, purpose, and hope as we navigate our journey of faith.

CHAPTER 03

ADAMIC DNA

The Origins of Humanity

The concept of Adamic DNA delves into the biblical narrative of creation, examining the genetic and spiritual heritage that traces back to Adam, the first human according to the Bible. Understanding Adamic DNA provides insights into humanity's physical and spiritual origins, the fall, and the redemptive plan of God. This chapter explores the implications of Adamic DNA on our identity, nature, and relationship with God.

The Creation of Adam

The story of Adam begins in Genesis 2:7 (NIV):

"Then the LORD God formed a man from the dust of the ground and breathed into his nostrils the breath of life, and the man became a living being."

This verse highlights two key aspects of human creation: the physical formation from the dust of the ground and the divine breath of life. Adam's DNA, therefore, represents a unique combination of earthly elements and divine essence, making him the prototype of human beings.

The Image of God

Genesis 1:27 (NIV) declares:

"So God created mankind in his own image, in the image of God he created them; male and female he created them."

Being made in the image of God signifies that humans carry divine attributes within their very being. This "Adamic DNA" encompasses not only physical traits but also spiritual characteristics such as the capacity for relationship, creativity, moral reasoning, and dominion over creation.

The Fall and Its Consequences

The narrative of Adam and Eve's disobedience in Genesis 3 profoundly impacts our understanding of Adamic DNA. Genesis 3:6 (NIV) recounts:

"When the woman saw that the fruit of the tree was good for food and pleasing to the eye, and also desirable for gaining wisdom, she took some and ate it. She also gave some to her husband, who was with her, and he ate it."

This act of disobedience, known as the Fall, introduced sin and its consequences into the human experience. Romans 5:12 (NIV) explains:

"Therefore, just as sin entered the world through one man, and death through sin, and in this way death came to all people, because all sinned."

The Fall corrupted the original purity of Adamic DNA, leading to spiritual and physical death, brokenness, and a propensity toward sin.

The Transmission of Sinful Nature

The concept of original sin suggests that the corrupted nature of Adam is inherited by all his descendants. Psalm 51:5 (NIV) reflects this reality:

"Surely I was sinful at birth, sinful from the time my mother conceived me."

This inherited sinful nature, often referred to as the "Adamic nature," means that every human is born with a predisposition to sin and separation from God.

Redemption Through the Second Adam

The New Testament presents Jesus Christ as the "Second Adam," who brings redemption and restoration. 1 Corinthians 15:21-22 (NIV) contrasts the two Adams:

"For since death came through a man, the resurrection of the dead comes also through a man. As in Adam all die, so in Christ, all will be made alive."

Jesus' sacrificial death and resurrection offer a way to overcome the effects of the Fall. Believers are invited to partake in a new spiritual DNA, characterized by righteousness and eternal life.

Spiritual Rebirth and New Creation

Through faith in Christ, individuals experience a spiritual rebirth, transforming their Adamic nature. John 3:3 (NIV) highlights this transformation:

"Jesus replied, 'Very truly I tell you, no one can see the kingdom of God unless they are born again.'"

This new birth signifies the infusion of divine life into the believer, creating a new spiritual identity. 2 Corinthians 5:17 (NIV) states:

"Therefore, if anyone is in Christ, the new creation has come: The old has gone, the new is here!"

This new creation reflects the restoration of the divine image and the renewal of our spiritual DNA.

Living Out the New Nature

Embracing the new spiritual DNA involves living according to the principles and values of God's kingdom. Ephesians 4:22-24 (NIV) encourages believers:

"You were taught, with regard to your former way of life, to put off your old self, which is being corrupted by its deceitful desires; to be made new in the attitude of your minds; and to put on the new self, created to be like God in true righteousness and holiness."

This transformation requires an ongoing commitment to spiritual growth, aligning our lives with the character of Christ.

The Hope of Glorification

The ultimate fulfillment of this transformation will occur at the resurrection when believers receive glorified bodies free from the effects of sin. Philippians 3:20-21 (NIV) promises:

"But our citizenship is in heaven. And we eagerly await a Savior from there, the Lord Jesus Christ, who, by the power that enables him to bring everything under his control, will transform our lowly bodies so that they will be like his glorious body."

This glorification represents the complete redemption of Adamic DNA, restoring humanity to its original glory and purpose.

Conclusion: Embracing Our Divine Heritage

Understanding Adamic DNA provides profound insights into our identity, nature, and destiny. While the Fall introduced sin and brokenness, the redemptive work of Christ offers a pathway to restoration and new life. By embracing our new spiritual DNA, we align ourselves with God's original design and purpose, living out the fullness of our divine heritage.

As we conclude this chapter, let us commit to embracing the new nature given to us through Christ, living in the light of His redemption, and looking forward to the ultimate glorification that awaits us. This journey of transformation reflects the ongoing work of God in our lives, restoring us to the fullness of His image and purpose.

CHAPTER 04

MASTER YOUR ALLEGIANCE IN GOD'S DNA

The Call to Allegiance

In a world where loyalties are often divided and distractions abound, mastering your allegiance to God is crucial for living a life that is aligned with His purpose and design. This chapter explores the concept of allegiance in the context of God's DNA, emphasizing the importance of unwavering commitment to God and how it shapes our identity, actions, and destiny.

Understanding Allegiance

Allegiance is defined as loyalty or commitment to a superior or to a cause. In the context of our relationship with God, it means placing Him at the center of our lives, making

His will and His Word the guiding principles of our existence. Joshua 24:15 (NIV) captures this commitment succinctly:

"But if serving the Lord seems undesirable to you, then choose for yourselves this day whom you will serve, whether the gods your ancestors served beyond the Euphrates, or the gods of the Amorites, in whose land you are living. But as for me and my household, we will serve the Lord."

This declaration by Joshua highlights the importance of making a deliberate choice to serve God above all else.

The Foundation of Allegiance in God's DNA

Our allegiance to God is rooted in our spiritual DNA, which reflects His image and likeness. Genesis 1:27 (NIV) states:

"So God created mankind in his own image, in the image of God he created them; male and female he created them."

Being made in God's image implies that our true identity and purpose are found in Him. This divine imprint forms the foundation of our allegiance, calling us to live in a way that honors and reflects our Creator.

Jesus as the Perfect Example

Jesus Christ provides the perfect example of unwavering allegiance to God. Throughout His life and ministry, Jesus demonstrated complete obedience and loyalty to the Father's will. John 6:38 (NIV) reveals Jesus' commitment:

"For I have come down from heaven not to do my will but to do the will of him who sent me."

Jesus' allegiance was evident in His actions, teachings, and ultimately His sacrifice on the cross. By following His example, we learn what it means to fully commit to God's purpose.

The Importance of Daily Commitment

Allegiance to God is not a one-time decision but a daily commitment. Luke 9:23 (NIV) underscores the necessity of daily dedication:

"Then he said to them all: 'Whoever wants to be my disciple must deny themselves and take up their cross daily and follow me.'"

Taking up our cross daily involves making choices that align with God's will, even when it is difficult or inconvenient. It requires a conscious effort to prioritize our relationship with God above all else.

Aligning with God's Word

Mastering our allegiance involves immersing ourselves in God's Word. Psalm 119:105 (NIV) highlights the guiding power of Scripture:

"Your word is a lamp for my feet, a light on my path."

By studying and meditating on the Bible, we gain clarity and direction for our lives. God's Word helps us understand His will, strengthens our resolve, and equips us to live according to His principles.

The Role of the Holy Spirit

The Holy Spirit plays a vital role in helping us maintain our allegiance to God. John 14:26 (NIV) promises the Spirit's guidance:

"But the Advocate, the Holy Spirit, whom the Father will send in my name, will teach you all things and will remind you of everything I have said to you."

The Holy Spirit empowers us to live faithfully, convicts us of sin, and guides us in truth. By relying on the Spirit, we can remain steadfast in our commitment to God.

Challenges to Allegiance

Maintaining allegiance to God can be challenging in a world filled with distractions and temptations. Ephesians 6:12-13 (NIV) reminds us of the spiritual battle we face:

"For our struggle is not against flesh and blood, but against the rulers, against the authorities, against the powers of this dark world and against the spiritual forces of evil in the heavenly realms. Therefore put on the full armor of God, so that when the day of evil comes, you may be able to stand your ground, and after you have done everything, to stand."

By putting on the full armor of God—truth, righteousness, faith, salvation, the Word of God, and prayer—we can withstand these challenges and remain loyal to our divine calling.

Practical Steps to Master Your Allegiance

1. Prioritize Prayer: Develop a consistent prayer life, seeking God's guidance and strength daily. Prayer keeps us connected to God and focused on His will.

2. Engage in Scripture: Regularly read and study the Bible. Reflect on its teachings and apply them to your life.

3. Stay Accountable: Surround yourself with a community of believers who encourage and hold you accountable in your faith journey.

4. Practice Obedience: Be intentional about obeying God's commands, even in small matters. Obedience builds spiritual discipline and reinforces your allegiance.

5. Seek the Holy Spirit's Help: Continually ask the Holy Spirit to fill you, guide you, and empower you to live according to God's will.

The Rewards of Allegiance

Living a life of allegiance to God brings profound rewards. John 15:5 (NIV) describes the fruitfulness that comes from abiding in Christ:

"I am the vine; you are the branches. If you remain in me and I in you, you will bear much fruit; apart from me you can do nothing."

By remaining faithful to God, we experience spiritual growth, deepened relationship with Him, and the fulfillment of His purpose in our lives.

Conclusion: Embracing Divine Allegiance

Mastering your allegiance in God's DNA is a journey of daily commitment, guided by Scripture and empowered by the Holy Spirit. By prioritizing your relationship with God and aligning your actions with His will, you reflect His image and fulfill His purpose for your life.

As we conclude this chapter, let us resolve to deepen our allegiance to God, embracing the divine DNA that defines our true identity and destiny. In doing so, we honor our Creator and experience the fullness of life He intends for us.

CHAPTER 05

THE DNA OF MAN: DID IT CHANGE YOUR LIFE?

The Marvel of Human DNA

Human DNA is a marvel of biological complexity and precision. This molecule, composed of a sequence of nucleotides, encodes the genetic instructions necessary for the growth, development, and functioning of every living organism. The discovery and understanding of DNA have revolutionized science, medicine, and our perception of life itself. In this chapter, we explore the profound impact of understanding human DNA on our lives, both scientifically and spiritually.

The Discovery of DNA

The discovery of DNA's structure in 1953 by James Watson and Francis Crick marked a significant milestone in the field of genetics. This breakthrough revealed the double helix structure of DNA, providing insights into how genetic information is stored, replicated, and transmitted. Understanding DNA has since paved the way for numerous advancements in medical research, genetic engineering, and biotechnology.

The Structure and Function of DNA

DNA, or deoxyribonucleic acid, consists of two long chains of nucleotides twisted into a double helix. Each nucleotide contains a sugar, a phosphate group, and a nitrogenous base (adenine, thymine, cytosine, or guanine). The sequence of these bases encodes genetic information, which is translated into proteins that perform various functions in the body.

The ability of DNA to replicate ensures that genetic information is passed from one generation to the next, maintaining continuity of life. Mutations, or changes in the DNA sequence, can lead to variations in traits and are the driving force behind evolution.

The Impact of DNA on Medicine

The understanding of DNA has had a profound impact on medicine. Genetic research has led to the identification of genes responsible for various hereditary diseases, enabling early diagnosis and personalized treatment. Techniques such as gene therapy, CRISPR-Cas9 gene editing, and genomic sequencing have opened new avenues for treating genetic disorders and improving health outcomes.

For instance, knowing one's genetic predisposition to certain diseases allows for proactive health management and personalized medical interventions. This knowledge has empowered individuals to make informed decisions about their health and lifestyle, ultimately enhancing their quality of life.

DNA and Personal Identity

Beyond its biological significance, DNA has profound implications for our understanding of personal identity. The uniqueness of an individual's DNA sequence underlines the distinctiveness of each person. This uniqueness extends to physical traits, susceptibility to diseases, and even aspects of personality and behavior.

Moreover, DNA testing has become a tool for exploring ancestry and heritage, allowing individuals to trace their lineage and understand their genetic roots. This connection to our ancestors can provide a sense of belonging and identity, enriching our understanding of who we are.

The Spiritual Dimension of DNA

From a spiritual perspective, the intricacy and complexity of DNA point to a divine Creator. Psalm 139:13-14 (NIV) reflects this sentiment:

"For you created my inmost being; you knit me together in my mother's womb. I praise you because I am fearfully and wonderfully made; your works are wonderful, I know that full well."

The belief that we are "fearfully and wonderfully made" underscores the idea that our genetic makeup is not random but purposefully designed. This perspective invites us to view our bodies as temples of the Holy Spirit, deserving of care and respect.

The Ethical Implications of Genetic Knowledge

The advancements in genetic research also bring ethical considerations. Issues such as genetic privacy, the potential for genetic discrimination, and the moral implications of gene editing challenge us to navigate the intersection of science and ethics thoughtfully. As stewards of this knowledge, we must ensure that it is used responsibly and equitably.

Personal Reflections: Did It Change Your Life?

Reflecting on the impact of understanding human DNA, one can see its transformative potential in both personal and broader contexts. For many, the knowledge of genetic predispositions has prompted lifestyle changes and proactive health measures. For others, the discovery of genetic links to ancestors has provided a deeper sense of identity and connection.

On a broader scale, the advancements in genetics have revolutionized healthcare, offering hope and solutions for previously incurable conditions. The ability to edit genes and potentially eradicate genetic disorders represents a monumental leap in human capability, raising hopes for a healthier future.

Conclusion: Embracing the Gift of DNA

The DNA of man is a testament to the complexity and beauty of life. Its discovery and understanding have not only revolutionized science and medicine but also deepened our appreciation for the divine design in our creation. By embracing the knowledge of our genetic makeup, we can make informed decisions about our health, explore our identity, and appreciate the intricate work of our Creator.

As we conclude this chapter, let us marvel at the wonder of DNA and its impact on our lives. Whether through scientific advancements or spiritual reflections, understanding our DNA invites us to live with greater awareness, purpose, and gratitude. It is a reminder that we are intricately designed, uniquely gifted, and called to steward the knowledge and resources entrusted to us for the betterment of ourselves and society.

CHAPTER 06

DISCOVERING YOUR TRUE SELF

The journey of self-discovery is one of the most profound and transformative experiences in life. It involves delving deep into our identity, understanding our purpose, and embracing the unique qualities that define us. This search for who we are is not just a quest for personal understanding but a spiritual journey that connects us with the divine blueprint embedded within us.

The Role of DNA in Self-Discovery

Our DNA is the fundamental blueprint of our physical being. It determines our physical traits, health predispositions, and even certain aspects of our behavior. Just as scientists decode the human genome to understand the intricacies of our biology, we must decode our spiritual DNA to uncover the deeper aspects of our identity. This involves recognizing the divine imprint within us, which shapes our moral and spiritual characteristics.

Biblical Insights into Identity

The Bible offers profound insights into our identity and purpose. One of the most compelling passages is Psalm 139:13-14 (NIV):

"For you created my inmost being; you knit me together in my mother's womb. I praise you because I am fearfully and wonderfully made; your works are wonderful, I know that full well."

This scripture emphasizes that our identity is intricately woven by God, affirming that we are purposefully and wonderfully made. Recognizing this divine craftsmanship is the first step in the search for who we are.

Understanding Your Spiritual DNA

Just as our physical DNA is unique to each individual, our spiritual DNA is a unique reflection of God's image within us. Genesis 1:27 (NIV) states:

"So God created mankind in his own image, in the image of God he created them; male and female he created them."

Being made in God's image means that we possess inherent qualities that reflect His nature, such as creativity, love, and moral reasoning. Understanding and embracing these qualities helps us to align with our true identity and purpose.

The Impact of Life Experiences

Our journey of self-discovery is also shaped by our life experiences. These experiences, whether positive or challenging, contribute to our growth and understanding of who we are. Romans 8:28 (NIV) reassures us:

"And we know that in all things God works for the good of those who love him, who have been called according to his purpose."

Even difficult experiences can serve as catalysts for personal and spiritual growth, helping us to uncover deeper layers of our identity and strengthen our relationship with God.

Embracing Your Unique Purpose

Each of us has a unique purpose that is aligned with our spiritual DNA. Ephesians 2:10 (NIV) highlights this:

"For we are God's handiwork, created in Christ Jesus to do good works, which God prepared in advance for us to do."

Understanding our purpose involves recognizing the specific talents and passions that God has placed within us.

By aligning our actions with these God-given gifts, we fulfill our unique role in the larger divine plan.

The Role of Community

Our search for identity is not meant to be a solitary journey. Community plays a crucial role in helping us discover and affirm who we are. Hebrews 10:24-25 (NIV) encourages us:

"And let us consider how we may spur one another on toward love and good deeds, not giving up meeting together, as some are in the habit of doing, but encouraging one another—and all the more as you see the Day approaching."

Engaging with a supportive community provides us with the encouragement, accountability, and wisdom needed to navigate our journey of self-discovery.

Practical Steps in the Search for Identity

1. Self-Reflection and Prayer: Spend time in self-reflection and prayer, asking God to reveal His purpose for your life. Journaling your thoughts and prayers can help clarify your understanding of who you are.

2. Engage with Scripture: Study biblical passages that speak about identity and purpose. Reflect on how these scriptures resonate with your personal experiences and beliefs.

3. Seek Guidance: Talk with trusted mentors, spiritual leaders, and friends who can provide insights and perspectives on your journey.

4. Embrace Your Gifts: Identify your talents and passions, and find ways to use them in service to others. This not only fulfills your purpose but also brings joy and satisfaction.

5. Practice Gratitude: Cultivate a habit of gratitude for the unique qualities and experiences that define you. Recognizing God's hand in your life fosters a deeper sense of identity and purpose.

Conclusion: Embracing Your True Self

The search for who you are is a lifelong journey that involves continuous growth and discovery. By understanding and embracing your spiritual DNA, you align yourself with the divine blueprint that God has crafted for your life. This journey is enriched by community, guided by scripture, and deepened through prayer and reflection. Ultimately, discovering who you are leads to a fulfilling and purposeful life that reflects the glory of God and His intricate design.

CHAPTER 07

THE POWER OF DIVINE PERSPECTIVE

In a world filled with varying opinions and perspectives, understanding and aligning with God's view can be transformative. God's opinions are not just arbitrary thoughts but profound truths that shape our reality. Embracing God's perspective means seeing ourselves and our world through His eyes, which can bring clarity, purpose, and peace.

The Foundation of God's Opinions

God's opinions are rooted in His character—His love, wisdom, and truth. Jeremiah 29:11 (NIV) encapsulates God's benevolent intentions:

"For I know the plans I have for you," declares the LORD, "plans to prosper you and not to harm you, plans to give you hope and a future."

This verse reveals that God's opinions are always for our good. They are designed to lead us toward a fulfilling and hopeful future. Understanding that God's thoughts are higher and more profound than our own is crucial in aligning our reality with His perspective.

Identity and Worth

One of the most significant aspects of God's opinion is His view of our identity and worth. Ephesians 2:10 (NIV) says:

"For we are God's handiwork, created in Christ Jesus to do good works, which God prepared in advance for us to do."

This verse affirms that we are God's masterpieces, created with intention and purpose. Our value is not determined by societal standards or personal achievements but by God's declaration that we are His beloved creation.

Overcoming Negative Self-Perceptions

Many people struggle with negative self-perceptions and feelings of inadequacy. God's opinion, however, is that we are fearfully and wonderfully made (Psalm 139:14 NIV). By embracing this divine truth, we can overcome the lies and negative self-talk that often plague our minds. Understanding that God sees us as valuable and capable can transform our self-perception and empower us to live confidently.

Purpose and Direction

God's opinions also provide clarity regarding our purpose and direction in life. Proverbs 3:5-6 (NIV) advises:

"Trust in the LORD with all your heart and lean not on your own understanding; in all your ways submit to him, and he will make your paths straight."

This scripture encourages us to rely on God's wisdom rather than our own understanding. By doing so, we align our paths with His divine purpose, ensuring that our steps are directed according to His perfect plan.

Facing Challenges with God's Perspective

Life's challenges can often skew our perception of reality. In times of difficulty, it is essential to remember Romans 8:28 (NIV):

"And we know that in all things God works for the good of those who love him, who have been called according to his purpose."

This promise reassures us that even in hardship, God is at work, orchestrating events for our ultimate good. By holding onto this truth, we can face challenges with a sense of peace and confidence, knowing that God's perspective is one of hope and redemption.

Transforming Our Minds

To fully embrace God's opinions as our reality, we must undergo a transformation of our minds. Romans 12:2 (NIV) instructs:

"Do not conform to the pattern of this world, but be transformed by the renewing of your mind. Then you will be able to test and approve what God's will is—his good, pleasing and perfect will."

Renewing our minds involves immersing ourselves in God's Word, meditating on His truths, and allowing His Spirit to reshape our thoughts and attitudes. This process enables us to discern and align with God's will, making His opinions the foundation of our reality.

Living Out God's Truths

Embracing God's opinions means actively living out the truths He has declared. James 1:22 (NIV) urges us:

"Do not merely listen to the word, and so deceive yourselves. Do what it says."

Living out God's truths involves applying His Word in our daily lives, making decisions based on His principles, and reflecting His character in our interactions with others. This practical application solidifies God's opinions as the guiding force in our reality.

Impact on Relationships

When we adopt God's perspective, it also transforms our relationships. Ephesians 4:32 (NIV) encourages:

"Be kind and compassionate to one another, forgiving each other, just as in Christ God forgave you."

Seeing others through God's eyes helps us to extend grace, forgiveness, and love. Recognizing that every person is valued and loved by God changes how we interact with them, fostering healthier and more meaningful relationships.

Conclusion: Embracing Divine Reality

Aligning our reality with God's opinions is a transformative journey that brings clarity, purpose, and peace. By embracing God's perspective on our identity, worth, purpose, and challenges, we can live confidently and purposefully. Transforming our minds through His Word and living out His truths solidify this divine reality in our lives.

Understanding that God's opinions are rooted in His love and wisdom helps us to trust and rely on Him fully. As we align our reality with His divine perspective, we experience the fullness of life He intends for us, marked by peace, purpose, and profound connection with Him.

CHAPTER 08

THE QUEST FOR APPROVAL

Stop Pondering for Approval

In today's world, the quest for approval can often overshadow our true purpose and identity. Whether seeking validation from peers, family, or society, this relentless pursuit can lead to a cycle of anxiety, self-doubt, and dissatisfaction. This chapter explores the importance of breaking free from the need for external approval and finding affirmation in God's unchanging love and acceptance.

The Nature of Approval-Seeking

Approval-seeking behavior is deeply ingrained in human nature. From a young age, we learn to seek praise and avoid criticism. This behavior can be beneficial in encouraging growth and development, but when it becomes the primary source of our self-worth, it can be detrimental. Galatians 1:10 (NIV) highlights the tension between seeking human approval and serving God:

"Am I now trying to win the approval of human beings, or of God? Or am I trying to please people? If I were still trying to please people, I would not be a servant of Christ."

This verse calls us to examine our motivations and prioritize God's approval over that of others.

The Illusion of Approval

The approval of others is often fleeting and conditional, based on ever-changing standards and expectations. It can lead to a constant state of insecurity, as we attempt to conform to the opinions and desires of those around us. Proverbs 29:25 (NIV) warns:

"Fear of man will prove to be a snare, but whoever trusts in the LORD is kept safe."

Relying on human approval traps us in a cycle of fear and instability while trusting in God provides security and peace.

Finding Approval in God

God's approval is unwavering and rooted in His unconditional love for us. Ephesians 1:4-5 (NIV) assures us:

"For he chose us in him before the creation of the world to be holy and blameless in his sight. In love, he predestined us for adoption to sonship through Jesus Christ, in accordance with his pleasure and will."

This passage reminds us that God's acceptance is not based on our performance but on His grace and love. Recognizing that we are chosen and loved by God frees us from the need to seek validation from others.

Living for an Audience of One

Colossians 3:23-24 (NIV) encourages us to shift our focus from pleasing people to serving God:

"Whatever you do, work at it with all your heart, as working for the Lord, not for human masters, since you know that you will receive an inheritance from the Lord as a reward. It is the Lord Christ you are serving."

Living for an audience of one means prioritizing God's approval in all aspects of our lives. This mindset transforms our actions and decisions, aligning them with God's will rather than human expectations.

The Freedom of God's Approval

Embracing God's approval brings freedom and peace. Romans 8:31-32 (NIV) declares:

"What, then, shall we say in response to these things? If God is for us, who can be against us? He who did not spare his own Son, but gave him up for us all—how will he not also, along with him, graciously give us all things?"

Knowing that God is for us eliminates the need to seek validation from others. His approval is sufficient, providing us with a solid foundation for our self-worth and identity.

Practical Steps to Stop Seeking Approval

1. Seek God's Perspective: Spend time in prayer and scripture, asking God to reveal His view of you. Meditate on verses that affirm your identity and worth in Christ.

2. Set Boundaries: Learn to say no to requests and expectations that are not aligned with your values and God's purpose for your life. Setting boundaries helps to protect your time, energy, and well-being.

3. Practice Gratitude: Cultivate a habit of gratitude for God's love and acceptance. Focus on the blessings and affirmations that come from Him rather than seeking them from others.

4. Surround Yourself with Supportive People: Engage with a community of believers who encourage and support you in your walk with God. Positive relationships can reinforce your identity in Christ and reduce the need for external validation.

5. Reflect on Your Motivations: Regularly examine your actions and decisions to ensure they are driven by a

desire to please God rather than gain human approval. Journaling can help you identify patterns and make necessary adjustments.

The Transformative Power of God's Approval

Embracing God's approval transforms our lives, allowing us to live authentically and purposefully. When we no longer seek validation from others, we are free to pursue God's calling and live in alignment with His will. This freedom brings joy, peace, and a deeper connection with God.

Conclusion: Embracing True Freedom

Stopping the relentless quest for human approval is a journey of embracing true freedom in Christ. By prioritizing God's approval and recognizing His unconditional love, we break free from the snares of seeking validation from others. Living for an audience of one allows us to fully embrace our identity and purpose, rooted in the unchanging love and acceptance of our Heavenly Father.

As we conclude this chapter, let us commit to seeking God's perspective and living for His glory. In doing so, we will experience the profound peace and freedom that comes from knowing we are fully accepted and loved by the Creator of the universe.

CHAPTER 09

THE POWER OF INTEGRITY

A Man of Your Words and Governed by Principles

In a world where promises are often broken and principles can be compromised, being a person of your word and governed by principles stands as a beacon of integrity and trustworthiness. This chapter explores the importance of living a life anchored in honesty, reliability, and unwavering moral principles, drawing inspiration from biblical teachings and practical examples.

The Value of Keeping Your Word

Keeping your word is fundamental to building trust and credibility. Proverbs 22:1 (NIV) emphasizes the value of a good reputation:

"A good name is more desirable than great riches; to be esteemed is better than silver or gold."

A reputation for honesty and reliability is priceless. When you consistently keep your promises, you build a legacy of trust that can positively impact every area of your life, from personal relationships to professional endeavors.

Biblical Foundation for Integrity

The Bible provides numerous examples and teachings on the importance of integrity. One of the most poignant is found in Matthew 5:37 (NIV), where Jesus instructs:

"All you need to say is simply 'Yes' or 'No'; anything beyond this comes from the evil one."

This directive underscores the importance of straightforwardness and reliability in our communication. Our words should be trustworthy and reflect our commitment to truth.

Living by Principles

Being governed by principles means adhering to a set of core values that guide your actions and decisions, regardless of the circumstances. Psalm 15:1-2 (NIV) describes the character of a person who is steadfast in their principles:

"Lord, who may dwell in your sacred tent? Who may live on your holy mountain? The one whose walk is blameless, who does what is righteous, who speaks the truth from their heart."

Principles such as honesty, fairness, compassion, and accountability form the foundation of a life of integrity. These values should inform every decision and action, ensuring consistency and moral clarity.

The Role of Faith in Integrity

Faith plays a crucial role in fostering integrity. Colossians 3:23-24 (NIV) encourages believers to work with sincerity:

"Whatever you do, work at it with all your heart, as working for the Lord, not for human masters, since you know that you will receive an inheritance from the Lord as a reward. It is the Lord Christ you are serving."

Understanding that our ultimate accountability is to God motivates us to live with integrity, knowing that our actions reflect our faith and commitment to Him.

Challenges to Integrity

Living a life of integrity is not without its challenges. Temptations to cut corners, tell white lies, or compromise on principles can be strong, especially when faced with immediate gains or pressures. Ephesians 6:11 (NIV) advises:

"Put on the full armor of God, so that you can take your stand against the devil's schemes."

Equipping ourselves with spiritual armor—truth, righteousness, faith, and the Word of God—enables us to resist these temptations and remain steadfast in our principles.

Practical Steps to Uphold Integrity

1. Commit to Honesty: Make a conscious decision to be truthful in all circumstances. This includes admitting mistakes, even when it's uncomfortable.

2. Align Actions with Values: Regularly reflect on your core values and ensure that your actions align with them. This alignment fosters consistency and authenticity.

3. Be Accountable: Seek accountability from trusted friends, mentors, or family members who can provide guidance and hold you to your commitments.

4. Practice Humility: Recognize that living with integrity is a continual process of growth. Be open to feedback and willing to make necessary changes.

5. Rely on God's Strength: Pray for the strength and wisdom to uphold your principles, especially in challenging situations. Philippians 4:13 (NIV) reassures us:

"I can do all this through him who gives me strength."

The Impact of Integrity

A life of integrity positively impacts not only the individual but also the wider community. Proverbs 11:3 (NIV) states:

"The integrity of the upright guides them, but the unfaithful are destroyed by their duplicity."

Your commitment to being a person of your word and governed by principles can inspire others, foster trust, and contribute to a culture of honesty and reliability.

Conclusion: Embracing a Life of Integrity

Living as a man of your words and governed by principles is a noble and fulfilling path. It requires dedication, self-discipline, and a steadfast commitment to truth and righteousness. By aligning your life with biblical teachings and core values, you build a foundation of trust and integrity that withstands the tests of time and circumstance.

As we conclude this chapter, let us commit to being individuals whose words are reliable and whose lives are governed by unwavering principles. By doing so, we not only honor God but also become a positive influence in our world, demonstrating the transformative power of a life rooted in integrity.

PART II

DNA IN THE BIBLE

CHAPTER 10

THE DIVINE BLUEPRINT

The Bible, written long before the discovery of DNA, often speaks of the intricate design and purpose behind creation. The complexity and precision we now understand in DNA echo the biblical descriptions of God's meticulous handiwork. Psalm 139:13-16 (NIV) provides a vivid depiction of this divine blueprint:

"For you created my inmost being; you knit me together in my mother's womb. I praise you because I am fearfully and wonderfully made; your works are wonderful, I know that full well. My frame was not hidden from you when I was made in the secret place when I was woven together in the depths of the earth. Your eyes saw my unformed body; all the days ordained for me were written in your book before one of them came to be."

This passage reflects the belief that God's hand is in every detail of our creation, akin to how DNA meticulously codes the blueprint for our physical form. The imagery of being "knit together" resonates with the precision and care involved in DNA's role in development.

God's Knowledge and Creation

Jeremiah 1:5 (NIV) further emphasizes the foreknowledge and intentionality of God in our creation:

"Before I formed you in the womb I knew you, before you were born I set you apart; I appointed you as a prophet to the nations."

This verse suggests that God's knowledge of us predates our physical formation, indicating a divine blueprint akin to DNA that defines our purpose and existence. The concept of being "known" before being formed implies an understanding that goes beyond the physical, touching on the spiritual essence encoded in our very being.

The Breath of Life

The creation narrative in Genesis provides a foundational perspective on the origin of life. Genesis 2:7 (NIV) describes the creation of man:

"Then the LORD God formed a man from the dust of the ground and breathed into his nostrils the breath of life, and the man became a living being."

This "breath of life" can be seen as a divine infusion, not just of physical life but of spiritual vitality, suggesting that our very essence is intertwined with God's spirit. The breath of life is akin to the activation of the genetic blueprint, transforming inanimate matter into a living, conscious being.

The Image of God

Genesis 1:27 (NIV) states:

"So God created mankind in his own image, in the image of God he created them; male and female he created them."

Being made in God's image signifies that there is something divine within our very being. This divine "DNA" implies that we carry a part of God's essence within us, a spiritual inheritance that transcends physical form. The concept of being created in God's image suggests that our genetic makeup, while unique to each individual, reflects a common divine origin.

The Continuity of Life

The Bible often speaks of the continuity of life, a concept mirrored in the perpetuation of genetic information through DNA. Ecclesiastes 1:4 (NIV) notes:

"Generations come and generations go, but the earth remains forever."

This continuity is paralleled in the transmission of DNA from generation to generation, ensuring the survival and propagation of life. Just as the earth remains a constant, so too does the genetic code that binds each generation to the next.

The Healing Power of God

The Bible frequently speaks of God's power to heal and restore, a concept that resonates with the body's intrinsic ability to repair DNA damage. Psalm 103:2-3 (NIV) declares:

"Praise the LORD, my soul, and forget not all his benefits—who forgives all your sins and heals all your diseases."

The body's ability to heal itself, including the repair mechanisms that correct DNA errors, can be seen as a reflection of God's restorative power. This healing is both physical and spiritual, encompassing the wholeness of our being.

Conclusion

The Bible, while written in a time without modern scientific knowledge, captures profound truths about the nature of life and creation that align with our understanding of DNA. The divine blueprint, the breath of life, the image of God, and the continuity of life all find echoes in the intricate design and function of DNA. By exploring these biblical insights, we gain a deeper appreciation of the divine hand in our creation and the spiritual dimensions of our genetic makeup. In the next chapter, we will delve into the relationship between DNA and human beings, further illuminating our connection with God.

CHAPTER 11

DNA AND HUMAN

The Blueprint of Life

Human DNA is like a complex blueprint that dictates everything about a person's physical characteristics, from eye color to susceptibility to certain diseases. This genetic information is stored in the sequence of the four chemical bases—adenine (A), guanine (G), cytosine (C), and thymine (T)—which form the rungs of the DNA double helix. Each person's unique combination of these bases determines their individual traits and functions.

Just as each cell in our body follows the instructions coded in our DNA, our spiritual life can be seen as following the divine blueprint set out by God. This blueprint not only shapes our physical form but also guides our spiritual journey, influencing our thoughts, actions, and relationship with the divine.

Relationship with God

The Bible often speaks of a personal relationship with God, likening it to the intimate connection of a father and his children. 1 John 3:1 (NIV) says:

"See what great love the Father has lavished on us, that we should be called children of God! And that is what we are!"

This relationship is more than metaphorical. Just as children inherit physical traits from their parents through DNA, we inherit spiritual traits from God, our Heavenly Father. This divine inheritance includes qualities such as love, compassion, and a sense of purpose, which are woven into our spiritual DNA.

Spiritual Inheritance

Romans 8:16-17 (NIV) states:

"The Spirit himself testifies with our spirit that we are God's children. Now if we are children, then we are heirs—heirs of God and co-heirs with Christ, if indeed we share in his sufferings in order that we may also share in his glory."

This inheritance is not just about material or physical traits but encompasses spiritual qualities and eternal life. As heirs of God, we are endowed with a spiritual legacy that guides us in our earthly journey and prepares us for our eternal destiny.

The Interconnectedness of Life

DNA not only connects us to our immediate family but also links us to our ancestors and future generations. This biological continuity mirrors the spiritual continuity described in the Bible. Hebrews 12:1 (NIV) speaks of a "great cloud of witnesses" surrounding us, suggesting a spiritual lineage that supports and encourages us:

"Therefore, since we are surrounded by such a great cloud of witnesses, let us throw off everything that hinders and the sin that so easily entangles. And let us run with perseverance the race marked out for us."

This interconnectedness underscores the idea that our lives are part of a larger tapestry, both biologically and spiritually, where each thread contributes to the overall pattern.

The Complexity and Precision of DNA

The precision and complexity of DNA, with its ability to encode vast amounts of information in a seemingly simple structure, reflect the wisdom and creativity of the Creator. The Bible celebrates this divine wisdom in passages like Job 38:4-7 (NIV), where God questions Job about the foundations of the earth:

"Where were you when I laid the earth's foundation? Tell me, if you understand. Who marked off its dimensions? Surely you know! Who stretched a measuring line across it? On what were its footings set, or who laid its cornerstone—while the morning stars sang together and all the angels shouted for joy?"

The intricacy of DNA serves as a reminder of the unfathomable knowledge and power of God, who designed all living beings with such meticulous care.

DNA and the Fall of Man

The Bible teaches that humanity's disobedience introduced sin and brokenness into the world. This concept can be seen metaphorically in the way mutations or errors in DNA can lead to diseases and disorders. Romans 5:12 (NIV) explains:

"Therefore, just as sin entered the world through one man, and death through sin, and in this way death came to all people because all sinned."

Just as sin disrupts our spiritual well-being, mutations disrupt the perfect functioning of our genetic code. Yet, just as there is redemption and healing in Christ, there are mechanisms within our cells designed to repair DNA damage, reflecting God's provision for restoration and wholeness.

Conclusion

Human DNA, with its intricate design and critical role in determining our physical and, metaphorically, our spiritual traits, serves as a powerful testament to the creativity and wisdom of God. Our genetic makeup connects us to our ancestors and future generations, much like our spiritual heritage connects us to God and the broader family of faith. By understanding DNA, we gain insights into the profound relationship between our physical existence and our spiritual journey, illuminating the divine blueprint that shapes our lives. In the next chapter, we will explore the spiritual dimension of DNA and how it reflects our connection to the divine.

CHAPTER 12

DNA: THE SPIRITUAL DIMENSION

God's Image and Likeness

The Bible tells us in Genesis 1:27 (NIV):

"So God created mankind in his own image, in the image of God he created them; male and female he created them."

Being made in God's image signifies that there is something divine within our very being. This divine "DNA" implies that we carry a part of God's essence within us, a spiritual inheritance that transcends physical form. Just as our physical DNA carries the genetic information that defines our biological characteristics, our spiritual DNA carries the imprint of God's nature, defining our capacity for love, compassion, creativity, and moral discernment.

The Breath of Life

Genesis 2:7 (NIV) describes the creation of man:

"Then the LORD God formed a man from the dust of the ground and breathed into his nostrils the breath of life, and the man became a living being."

This "breath of life" can be seen as a divine infusion, not just of physical life but of spiritual vitality. It suggests that our very essence is intertwined with God's spirit. This breath, akin to a spiritual code, activates the potential within us, much like how DNA activates the development and functioning of our physical bodies.

The Spiritual Blueprint

Our spiritual DNA, so to speak, contains the blueprint for our growth and development as spiritual beings. It guides us towards love, compassion, and a deeper connection with God. Romans 8:16-17 (NIV) states:

"The Spirit himself testifies with our spirit that we are God's children. Now if we are children, then we are heirs—heirs of God and co-heirs with Christ, if indeed we share in his sufferings in order that we may also share in his glory."

This inheritance of spiritual qualities enables us to reflect God's character in our lives, shaping our actions and guiding our moral compass. Just as physical DNA determines our biological traits, our spiritual DNA influences our capacity for empathy, kindness, and righteousness.

Transformation and Renewal

The New Testament speaks of transformation and renewal, concepts that resonate with the idea of spiritual DNA. 2 Corinthians 5:17 (NIV) declares:

"Therefore, if anyone is in Christ, the new creation has come: The old has gone, the new is here!"

This transformation signifies a renewal of our spiritual DNA, where the old sinful nature is replaced with a new nature aligned with God's will. This process of renewal is ongoing, much like the continuous replication and repair of DNA within our cells, ensuring that our spiritual growth and development remain aligned with the divine blueprint.

The Role of the Holy Spirit

The Holy Spirit plays a crucial role in shaping and nurturing our spiritual DNA. Galatians 5:22-23 (NIV) describes the fruit of the Spirit:

"But the fruit of the Spirit is love, joy, peace, forbearance, kindness, goodness, faithfulness, gentleness and self-control. Against such things there is no law."

These qualities, produced by the Holy Spirit, are the markers of our spiritual DNA. They are the evidence of God's presence within us, guiding us to live according to His purpose and reflecting His nature in our daily lives.

Spiritual Inheritance and Growth

Our spiritual DNA not only defines our current state but also our potential for growth and development. Ephesians 4:15-16 (NIV) encourages believers to grow in their faith:

"Instead, speaking the truth in love, we will grow to become in every respect the mature body of him who is the head, that is, Christ. From him the whole body, joined and held together by every supporting ligament, grows and builds itself up in love, as each part does its work."

This growth is facilitated by our spiritual DNA, which provides the foundation for developing deeper faith, stronger relationships, and a more profound understanding of God's will.

The Eternal Perspective

Finally, our spiritual DNA has an eternal dimension. John 3:16 (NIV) promises eternal life to those who believe in Jesus:

"For God so loved the world that he gave his one and only Son, that whoever believes in him shall not perish but have eternal life."

This eternal perspective highlights that our spiritual DNA is not confined to our earthly existence but extends into eternity, offering the promise of everlasting life with God.

Conclusion

Understanding the spiritual dimension of DNA enriches our appreciation of the divine blueprint that shapes our existence. Our spiritual DNA, imbued with God's image and infused with His breath of life, guides our growth, transformation, and eternal destiny. By embracing this spiritual inheritance, we can live more fully in alignment with God's purpose, reflecting His nature in our lives and nurturing our relationship with the divine. In the next chapter, we will explore why DNA is inherently spiritual and how this understanding deepens our connection with God.

CHAPTER 13

WHY DNA IS SPIRITUAL?

The Breath of Life

The concept of DNA as spiritual begins with the very breath of life given by God. Genesis 2:7 (NIV) describes the creation of man:

"Then the LORD God formed a man from the dust of the ground and breathed into his nostrils the breath of life, and the man became a living being."

This divine act of breathing life into Adam signifies more than just physical existence; it represents the infusion of a spiritual essence into humanity. Just as DNA serves as the blueprint for physical life, this breath of life serves as the blueprint for our spiritual existence, intertwining our very being with the divine.

A Living Connection

Our DNA connects us to our ancestors and future generations, forming a continuous line of life. Similarly, our spiritual DNA connects us to God, forming an unbroken bond of divine love and purpose. John 15:5 (NIV) illustrates this connection:

"I am the vine; you are the branches. If you remain in me and I in you, you will bear much fruit; apart from me you can do nothing."

This living connection is vital for our spiritual nourishment and growth, just as DNA is essential for our biological functions. It signifies that our spiritual life is not an isolated journey but one that is deeply rooted in our relationship with God.

The Image of God

Being made in God's image, as stated in Genesis 1:27 (NIV):

"So God created mankind in his own image, in the image of God he created them; male and female he created them."

This means that our spiritual DNA carries the imprint of the divine. This spiritual inheritance is not just about our physical resemblance to God but our moral and spiritual capacity to reflect His character. Our ability to love, create, reason, and choose aligns with the divine attributes we have inherited.

The Transformative Power of Spiritual DNA

The transformative power of spiritual DNA is akin to the biological process where our genetic code determines our growth and development. 2 Corinthians 5:17 (NIV) speaks of the transformation in Christ:

"Therefore, if anyone is in Christ, the new creation has come: The old has gone, the new is here!"

This transformation signifies a renewal of our spiritual DNA, where the old sinful nature is replaced with a new nature aligned with God's will. The process of sanctification, much like the continuous replication and repair of DNA, ensures that our spiritual growth remains aligned with the divine blueprint.

Healing and Restoration

Just as our physical DNA contains mechanisms to repair and restore genetic damage, our spiritual DNA has the capacity for healing and restoration through God's grace. Psalm 103:2-3 (NIV) declares:

"Praise the LORD, my soul, and forget not all his benefits—who forgives all your sins and heals all your diseases."

This healing is both physical and spiritual, encompassing the wholeness of our being. The forgiveness of sins and the healing of diseases reflect the restorative power inherent in our spiritual DNA, enabled by God's love and mercy.

The Eternal Perspective

Our spiritual DNA has an eternal dimension that transcends our earthly existence. John 3:16 (NIV) promises eternal life to those who believe in Jesus:

"For God so loved the world that he gave his one and only Son, that whoever believes in him shall not perish but have eternal life."

This eternal perspective underscores that our spiritual DNA is not confined to temporal boundaries but extends into eternity. It offers the promise of everlasting life with God, highlighting the profound spiritual significance of our divine inheritance.

Purpose and Calling

Our spiritual DNA also defines our purpose and calling in life. Ephesians 2:10 (NIV) states:

"For we are God's handiwork, created in Christ Jesus to do good works, which God prepared in advance for us to do."

This verse underscores that our lives are not random but are imbued with divine purpose. Our spiritual DNA equips us to fulfill the unique calling God has placed on each of our lives, guiding us to live out the good works He has prepared for us.

Conclusion

DNA is inherently spiritual because it reflects the divine blueprint that shapes our existence, both physically and spiritually. The breath of life, the image of God, the living connection with the divine, and the transformative power of spiritual DNA all point to a profound relationship between our genetic makeup and our spiritual essence. By embracing this understanding, we deepen our connection with God and live more fully in alignment with His purpose for us. This spiritual dimension of DNA illuminates the divine hand in our creation and guides us on our journey toward eternal life with Him.

CHAPTER 14

EMBRACING GOD'S DNA

Understanding DNA from both a scientific and spiritual perspective enriches our appreciation of the complexity and beauty of life. DNA, with its intricate coding and precise functioning, serves as a powerful testament to the wisdom and creativity of the Creator. This divine blueprint not only shapes our physical characteristics but also guides our spiritual journey, reflecting our connection with God.

The Divine Blueprint

As we have explored throughout this book, DNA is more than just a biological molecule; it is a symbol of the divine blueprint that underpins our existence. Psalm 139:13-14 (NIV) beautifully encapsulates this idea:

"For you created my inmost being; you knit me together in my mother's womb. I praise you because I am fearfully and wonderfully made; your works are wonderful, I know that full well."

This passage reminds us that every aspect of our being is crafted with purpose and care by God. Our DNA is a testament to His meticulous design, a reflection of His hand in every detail of our creation.

The Spiritual Dimension

Our exploration of DNA's spiritual dimension has revealed profound insights into our relationship with God. Being made in God's image, infused with His breath of life, and connected to Him through our spiritual DNA, we carry a part of His essence within us. This divine inheritance shapes our moral and spiritual capacities, guiding us toward love, compassion, and a deeper connection with the divine.

Living the Divine Blueprint

Embracing God's DNA means recognizing and living according to this divine blueprint. It involves aligning our lives with the spiritual qualities and purposes God has woven into our very being. Romans 12:2 (NIV) encourages us:

"Do not conform to the pattern of this world, but be transformed by the renewing of your mind. Then you will be able to test and approve what God's will is—his good, pleasing and perfect will."

By renewing our minds and hearts, we allow God's spiritual DNA to transform us, enabling us to live out His will and reflect His nature in our daily lives.

The Promise of Eternal Life

Our spiritual DNA also carries the promise of eternal life. John 3:16 (NIV) assures us:

"For God so loved the world that he gave his one and only Son, that whoever believes in him shall not perish but have eternal life."

This promise extends our understanding of DNA beyond the physical realm, offering a vision of eternal connection with God. Our spiritual journey, guided by the divine blueprint, leads us toward this ultimate fulfillment.

A Call to Reflection and Action

In light of this profound connection between our DNA and our spiritual life, we are called to reflect deeply on our identity and purpose. We are invited to embrace our divine heritage and live in a way that honors the intricate design God has placed within us. Colossians 3:17 (NIV) provides a guiding principle:

"And whatever you do, whether in word or deed, do it all in the name of the Lord Jesus, giving thanks to God the Father through him."

By living with this mindset, we acknowledge and celebrate the divine DNA that shapes us, using our unique gifts and abilities to glorify God and serve others.

Final Thoughts

Embracing God's DNA means recognizing the divine blueprint that guides our physical and spiritual existence. It involves understanding our identity as children of God, created in His image, and living according to the spiritual inheritance we have received. This journey of discovery and transformation is one of deepening our connection with God, fulfilling our purpose, and embracing the promise of eternal life.

As we conclude this exploration, may we be inspired to live fully in the light of God's design, celebrating the divine DNA that makes us fearfully and wonderfully made, both in body and spirit.

CHAPTER 15

THE RELATIONSHIP BETWEEN GOD'S DNA AND HUMAN DNA

The Divine Connection

The concept of DNA, the fundamental building block of life, is a marvel of biological science. However, when we explore DNA through a biblical lens, we uncover a profound connection between our genetic makeup and our spiritual essence. This chapter delves into the relationship between God's DNA and human DNA, using biblical references to illuminate this divine connection.

The Creation of Humanity

The Bible provides a foundational perspective on the creation of humanity. Genesis 1:27 (NIV) states:

"So God created mankind in his own image, in the image of God he created them; male and female he created them."

This verse highlights that humans are created in the image of God, indicating a unique relationship between the Creator and His creation. This divine image can be seen as a reflection of God's spiritual DNA within us, encompassing our capacity for relationship, morality, and creativity.

The Breath of Life

Genesis 2:7 (NIV) further describes the intimate act of creation:

"Then the LORD God formed a man from the dust of the ground and breathed into his nostrils the breath of life, and the man became a living being."

The breath of life from God signifies not just physical life but the infusion of spiritual vitality. This divine breath is akin to spiritual DNA, embedding within us the essence of God's own life. It signifies that our existence is both physical and spiritual, intertwining the two in a holistic unity.

The Divine Blueprint

Psalm 139:13-14 (NIV) beautifully captures the intricacy of God's design:

"For you created my inmost being; you knit me together in my mother's womb. I praise you because I am fearfully and wonderfully made; your works are wonderful, I know that full well."

The intricate knitting together of our being reflects the detailed coding of DNA. Just as DNA contains the genetic blueprint for our physical development, God's design encompasses both our physical and spiritual attributes, highlighting the comprehensive nature of His creation.

The Fall and Its Impact

The narrative of the Fall in Genesis 3 introduces sin and its consequences into the human experience. Romans 5:12 (NIV) explains:

"Therefore, just as sin entered the world through one man, and death through sin, and in this way death came to all people, because all sinned."

The introduction of sin corrupted the original purity of human DNA, leading to spiritual death and separation from God. This spiritual corruption is passed down through generations, much like genetic traits, indicating a profound connection between our physical and spiritual inheritance.

Redemption Through Christ

The New Testament presents Jesus Christ as the means of redemption, offering a pathway to restore the corrupted spiritual DNA. 1 Corinthians 15:21-22 (NIV) contrasts the two Adams:

"For since death came through a man, the resurrection of the dead comes also through a man. For as in Adam all die, so in Christ all will be made alive."

Through Jesus' sacrifice and resurrection, believers are given the opportunity to receive a new spiritual identity, characterized by righteousness and eternal life. This redemption process signifies a renewal of our spiritual DNA, aligning it once again with God's original design.

Spiritual Rebirth and New Creation

Jesus emphasizes the necessity of spiritual rebirth in John 3:3 (NIV):

"Jesus replied, 'Very truly I tell you, no one can see the kingdom of God unless they are born again.'"

This rebirth signifies the transformation of our spiritual DNA. 2 Corinthians 5:17 (NIV) affirms:

"Therefore, if anyone is in Christ, the new creation has come: The old has gone, the new is here!"

This transformation is the essence of living out our new spiritual identity, reflecting God's character and purpose.

Living Out the Divine DNA

Ephesians 4:22-24 (NIV) instructs believers on living according to their new nature:

"You were taught, with regard to your former way of life, to put off your old self, which is being corrupted by its deceitful desires; to be made new in the attitude of your minds; and to put on the new self, created to be like God in true righteousness and holiness."

Living out the divine DNA involves embracing the new spiritual identity given through Christ and aligning our lives with God's principles. It requires daily commitment to righteousness and holiness, reflecting the image of God in our actions and decisions.

The Role of the Holy Spirit

The Holy Spirit plays a crucial role in helping us live out our divine DNA. Romans 8:14-16 (NIV) highlights this relationship:

"For those who are led by the Spirit of God are the children of God. The Spirit you received does not make you slaves, so that you live in fear again; rather, the Spirit you received brought about your adoption to sonship. And by him we cry, 'Abba, Father.' The Spirit himself testifies with our spirit that we are God's children."

The Holy Spirit guides, empowers, and confirms our identity as children of God, enabling us to reflect His character and fulfill His purpose.

Conclusion: Embracing the Divine Connection

Understanding the relationship between God's DNA and human DNA provides a profound insight into our identity and purpose. By recognizing the divine imprint in our creation, the impact of sin, and the redemptive power of Christ, we can embrace our spiritual DNA and live out God's blueprint for our lives.

As we conclude this chapter, let us reflect on the transformative power of this divine connection. By aligning our lives with God's Word and embracing our new identity in Christ, we can experience the fullness of life that God intends for us. This understanding not only changes our perception of ourselves but also empowers us to live with greater purpose, integrity, and devotion to our Creator.

PART III

FORENSIC DNA

CHAPTER 16

THE POWER OF DNA IN FORENSIC SCIENCE

The Revolution of DNA in Forensics

DNA, the molecule that carries genetic information, has revolutionized the field of forensic science. Its ability to uniquely identify individuals has transformed how crimes are investigated and solved, providing powerful tools for law enforcement and the judicial system. This chapter explores the power of DNA in forensic science, its applications, methodologies, and impact on criminal justice.

The Basics of DNA

Deoxyribonucleic acid (DNA) is a long molecule that contains our unique genetic code. It is found in almost every cell of the human body. DNA is composed of four chemical bases: adenine (A), thymine (T), cytosine (C), and guanine (G). These bases pair up (A with T, and C with G) to form units called base pairs, which make up the double helix structure of DNA. The sequence of these bases determines the genetic information available for building and maintaining an organism.

The Introduction of DNA in Forensics

The use of DNA in forensic science began in the mid-1980s. The landmark case that brought DNA to the forefront of forensic science was the 1986 case of Colin Pitchfork in the UK. DNA profiling, also known as genetic fingerprinting, was used to convict Pitchfork of rape and murder, establishing DNA as a powerful tool in forensic investigations.

DNA Profiling Methods

1. Short Tandem Repeats (STRs):

STR analysis is the most common method used in forensic DNA profiling. STRs are short sequences of DNA that are repeated at specific locations in the genome. The number of repeats varies between individuals, making STRs highly useful for identification. By analyzing multiple STR loci, forensic scientists can create a DNA profile that is statistically unique to an individual.

2. Mitochondrial DNA (mtDNA):

Mitochondrial DNA is inherited only from the mother and is present in the mitochondria of cells. It is used in cases where nuclear DNA is not available, such as in old or degraded samples. mtDNA analysis is useful for identifying remains by comparing the mtDNA profile to that of maternal relatives.

3. Y-Chromosome Analysis:

This method targets the Y-chromosome, which is passed from father to son. It is particularly useful in cases involving male lineage, such as paternity testing and cases of sexual assault where the suspect is male.

4. Single Nucleotide Polymorphisms (SNPs):

SNPs are variations at a single base pair in the DNA sequence. They are less variable than STRs but can provide valuable information, especially in complex cases or degraded samples. SNP analysis can also provide insights into ancestry and physical traits.

Applications of DNA in Forensic Science

1. Crime Scene Investigation:

DNA evidence collected from crime scenes, such as blood, hair, skin cells, or bodily fluids, can be used to identify suspects or victims. The DNA profile generated from the evidence can be compared to profiles in databases or from potential suspects to find matches.

2. Cold Cases:

DNA technology has been instrumental in solving cold cases. Advances in DNA analysis and the ability to analyze degraded samples have allowed investigators to revisit unsolved cases and identify perpetrators years after the crime was committed.

3. Exoneration of the Innocent:

DNA evidence has played a crucial role in exonerating individuals wrongfully convicted of crimes. Organizations like the Innocence Project use DNA testing to reexamine evidence and prove the innocence of those who were falsely accused and convicted.

4. Identification of Human Remains:

DNA profiling is used to identify human remains in cases of missing persons, mass disasters, and unidentified bodies. By comparing the DNA profile of the remains to that of known relatives, forensic scientists can establish the identity of the deceased.

5. Paternity and Kinship Testing:

DNA testing is commonly used in paternity and kinship cases to determine biological relationships. This has applications in legal disputes, immigration cases, and inheritance claims.

Challenges and Limitations

While DNA has revolutionized forensic science, it is not without challenges and limitations. These include:

1. Contamination:

DNA samples can be easily contaminated by handling or environmental factors. Strict protocols must be followed to prevent contamination and ensure the integrity of the evidence.

2. Degraded Samples:

DNA degrades over time, especially in harsh environmental conditions. Advanced techniques and methods are needed to analyze degraded samples and obtain usable profiles.

3. Interpretation of Mixed Samples:

Crime scenes often contain mixed DNA samples from multiple individuals. Interpreting these mixtures can be complex and requires sophisticated software and expertise.

4. Privacy Concerns:

The collection and storage of DNA profiles raise privacy and ethical concerns. There is ongoing debate about the balance between public safety and individual privacy rights.

Conclusion: The Transformative Power of DNA in Forensics

The power of DNA in forensic science cannot be overstated. It has transformed the way crimes are investigated and solved, providing a reliable and powerful tool for identifying individuals, solving cold cases, exonerating the innocent, and identifying human remains. Despite challenges and limitations, the advancements in DNA technology continue to enhance the accuracy and efficiency of forensic investigations.

As we conclude this chapter, it is evident that DNA's role in forensic science has not only changed the landscape of criminal justice but has also had a profound impact on society. By leveraging the power of DNA, we can pursue justice with greater precision and ensure that the truth prevails in the pursuit of justice.

CHAPTER 17

THE SPIRITUAL DIMENSION OF DNA IN FORENSIC SCIENCE

The Intersection of Science and Spirituality

Forensic science, particularly through the use of DNA, has significantly impacted the field of criminal justice. While DNA analysis is fundamentally a scientific endeavor, it also has profound spiritual implications. This chapter explores how DNA in forensic science can be seen through a spiritual lens, highlighting the deeper meanings and ethical considerations that arise when science and spirituality intersect.

The Divine Blueprint

DNA is often described as the blueprint of life, containing the genetic instructions that guide the development and functioning of every living organism. From a spiritual perspective, this intricate design reflects the handiwork of a Creator. Psalm 139:13-14 (NIV) eloquently captures this idea:

"For you created my inmost being; you knit me together in my mother's womb. I praise you because I am fearfully and wonderfully made; your works are wonderful, I know that full well."

The complexity and precision of DNA point to divine intelligence, suggesting that our very essence is crafted with purpose and care. In forensic science, the ability to analyze DNA and uncover hidden truths can be seen as an extension of understanding this divine blueprint.

The Search for Truth

Forensic science is fundamentally about seeking truth. In criminal investigations, DNA evidence helps to uncover facts, identify perpetrators, and exonerate the innocent. This pursuit of truth aligns with spiritual principles. John 8:32 (NIV) states:

"Then you will know the truth, and the truth will set you free."

The process of uncovering the truth through DNA analysis can be seen as a manifestation of a higher calling to justice and righteousness. By bringing clarity and resolution to complex cases, forensic science serves a noble purpose that resonates with spiritual values.

Justice and Redemption

The use of DNA in forensic science plays a critical role in the pursuit of justice. It helps to hold the guilty accountable and provides a pathway for the innocent to be exonerated. This aligns with the biblical principle of justice, as seen in Isaiah 1:17 (NIV):

"Learn to do right; seek justice. Defend the oppressed. Take up the cause of the fatherless; plead the case of the widow."

Furthermore, the exoneration of wrongfully convicted individuals through DNA evidence echoes the theme of redemption found throughout Scripture. The ability to correct wrongful convictions and restore individuals to their rightful place reflects the redemptive nature of God's justice.

Ethical Considerations and Respect for Life

The collection and analysis of DNA in forensic science raise important ethical considerations. Respecting the sanctity of life and the dignity of individuals is paramount. Genesis 1:27 (NIV) emphasizes the inherent value of every person:

"So God created mankind in his own image, in the image of God he created them; male and female he created them."

This perspective calls for the ethical use of DNA evidence, ensuring that it is collected, analyzed, and used in ways that honor the dignity and rights of individuals. Ethical considerations include issues of consent, privacy, and the potential for misuse of genetic information.

Healing and Closure

For families affected by crime, the identification of victims through DNA analysis can bring a sense of closure and healing. The ability to provide answers and resolve uncertainties aligns with the biblical theme of bringing comfort to those who mourn. Matthew 5:4 (NIV) states:

"Blessed are those who mourn, for they will be comforted."

The spiritual dimension of forensic science lies in its potential to bring peace and solace to grieving families, allowing them to find closure and begin the healing process.

Stewardship of Knowledge

The advancements in DNA technology represent significant progress in human understanding and capability. As stewards of this knowledge, we are called to use it responsibly and ethically. Proverbs 2:6 (NIV) reminds us:

"For the Lord gives wisdom; from his mouth come knowledge and understanding."

This verse encourages us to seek wisdom and guidance in the application of scientific advancements, ensuring that our actions align with ethical and spiritual principles.

Connecting with the Divine

The process of analyzing DNA and uncovering the mysteries of life can also be a deeply spiritual experience for those involved in forensic science. Recognizing the divine complexity within every strand of DNA can inspire awe and reverence for the Creator. Romans 1:20 (NIV) reflects this sentiment:

"For since the creation of the world God's invisible qualities—his eternal power and divine nature—have been clearly seen, being understood from what has been made, so that people are without excuse."

This perspective invites forensic scientists to view their work as a form of worship, acknowledging the divine intelligence behind the genetic code and striving to honor that through their pursuit of truth and justice.

Conclusion: Embracing the Spiritual Dimension

The power of DNA in forensic science extends beyond its scientific applications, touching on profound spiritual truths and ethical considerations. By recognizing the divine blueprint within our genetic makeup, seeking truth and justice, and respecting the dignity of individuals, we can align the practice of forensic science with spiritual principles.

As we conclude this chapter, let us embrace the spiritual dimension of DNA in forensic science, acknowledging the divine craftsmanship behind every strand of DNA and committing to use this knowledge in ways that honor and reflect our Creator. In doing so, we can ensure that our pursuit of scientific truth also upholds the highest ethical and spiritual standards, serving the greater good and fulfilling our calling to justice and righteousness.

CHAPTER 18

JESUS AS THE WAY AND TRUTH: A COMPARISON WITH FORENSIC SCIENCE IN SOLVING PROBLEMS

Introduction: The Quest for Truth

Forensic science and the teachings of Jesus Christ share a common goal: the pursuit of truth. Forensic science seeks to uncover facts and bring clarity to complex situations, while Jesus declared Himself to be the way, the truth, and the life. This chapter explores the parallels between Jesus' role in guiding us to truth and the role of forensic science in solving problems, using biblical verses as a foundation.

Jesus as the Way, the Truth, and the Life

In John 14:6 (NIV), Jesus makes a profound declaration:

"Jesus answered, 'I am the way and the truth and the life. No one comes to the Father except through me.'"

This statement encapsulates the essence of Jesus' mission. He is the path to spiritual truth, the embodiment of divine truth, and the source of eternal life. Just as forensic science seeks to reveal the truth in criminal investigations, Jesus provides the ultimate truth in our spiritual journey.

The Role of Forensic Science

Forensic science plays a critical role in the criminal justice system by analyzing evidence to solve crimes. It involves the meticulous collection, examination, and interpretation of physical evidence to uncover the facts and bring justice. The objective nature of forensic science ensures that truth is revealed based on evidence rather than speculation or bias.

Uncovering Hidden Truths

One of the primary functions of forensic science is to uncover hidden truths. Similarly, Jesus' teachings reveal deeper spiritual truths that are often hidden from human understanding. In Luke 8:17 (NIV), Jesus says:

"For there is nothing hidden that will not be disclosed, and nothing concealed that will not be known or brought out into the open."

Both forensic science and Jesus' teachings emphasize the importance of bringing hidden truths to light, whether they pertain to solving a crime or understanding spiritual realities.

Providing Clarity and Direction

Forensic science provides clarity in legal cases by using scientific methods to analyze evidence and draw conclusions. Jesus, as the way, offers clarity and direction in our lives. Proverbs 3:5-6 (NIV) advises:

"Trust in the LORD with all your heart and lean not on your own understanding; in all your ways submit to him, and he will make your paths straight."

Just as forensic science relies on systematic analysis to provide clear answers, following Jesus' guidance helps us navigate life's complexities with confidence and purpose.

The Pursuit of Justice

Forensic science seeks to ensure justice by identifying perpetrators and exonerating the innocent. This pursuit of justice aligns with biblical principles. Isaiah 1:17 (NIV) calls us to:

"Learn to do right; seek justice. Defend the oppressed. Take up the cause of the fatherless; plead the case of the widow."

Jesus' ministry also emphasized justice, compassion, and righteousness. In John 8:32 (NIV), He says:

"Then you will know the truth, and the truth will set you free."

The liberation that comes from knowing the truth parallels the freedom that forensic science can bring to those wrongfully accused or seeking justice.

Restoring Peace and Order

The resolution of criminal cases through forensic science brings peace and order to society. Similarly, Jesus' mission was to restore peace and order to a fallen world. Colossians 1:19-20 (NIV) states:

"For God was pleased to have all his fullness dwell in him, and through him to reconcile to himself all things, whether things on earth or things in heaven, by making peace through his blood, shed on the cross."

Both forensic science and the redemptive work of Jesus aim to restore harmony and rectify wrongs, whether in the physical realm or the spiritual.

Transformative Power

The application of forensic science can transform lives by bringing closure to victims and holding offenders accountable. Likewise, the transformative power of Jesus' truth changes lives on a spiritual level. Romans 12:2 (NIV) encourages:

"Do not conform to the pattern of this world, but be transformed by the renewing of your mind. Then you will be able to test and approve what God's will is—his good, pleasing, and perfect will."

The renewal and transformation offered by Jesus mirror the restorative impact of forensic science in the pursuit of justice and truth.

Ethical Considerations

Both forensic science and following Jesus require adherence to ethical standards. Forensic scientists must operate with integrity, ensuring that their work is unbiased and accurate. Similarly, Jesus taught the importance of ethical behavior and integrity. Matthew 5:37 (NIV) instructs:

"All you need to say is simply 'Yes' or 'No'; anything beyond this comes from the evil one."

The commitment to truth and integrity is essential in both disciplines, ensuring that justice and righteousness prevail.

Conclusion: The Convergence of Science and Spirituality

The comparison between Jesus as the way and truth and forensic science reveals a profound convergence of science and spirituality in the pursuit of truth and justice. Both seek to uncover hidden truths, provide clarity, ensure justice, and transform lives. By understanding these parallels, we gain a deeper appreciation for the role of truth in both our spiritual journey and the criminal justice system.

As we conclude this chapter, let us recognize the transformative power of truth, whether revealed through forensic science or the teachings of Jesus. Embracing this truth leads to justice, peace, and a deeper connection with the divine, guiding us to live with integrity and purpose in all aspects of our lives.

CHAPTER 19

CONCLUDING THE BOOK OF GOD'S DNA AND ITS IMPORTANCE IN UNDERSTANDING GOD

Introduction: Reflecting on the Journey

As we conclude our exploration of "God's DNA," it is essential to reflect on the profound insights we have gained about our identity, purpose, and relationship with the divine. Understanding God's DNA has provided us with a deeper appreciation of how intricately and purposefully we are created. This final chapter will summarize key themes and highlight the importance of understanding God's DNA in our spiritual journey.

The Divine Blueprint: God's Image in Us

From the outset, we established that humans are created in the image of God, a concept central to understanding God's DNA. Genesis 1:27 (NIV) states:

"So God created mankind in his own image, in the image of God he created them; male and female he created them."

This divine imprint is not merely a physical resemblance but encompasses our moral, spiritual, and relational capacities. Recognizing that we bear God's image elevates our sense of self-worth and responsibility, reminding us that we are called to reflect God's character in our lives.

The Fall and Redemption: The Role of Adamic DNA

The concept of Adamic DNA, representing our fallen nature, underscores the reality of sin and its impact on humanity. Romans 5:12 (NIV) explains:

"Therefore, just as sin entered the world through one man, and death through sin, and in this way death came to all people because all sinned."

Understanding Adamic DNA helps us comprehend the human condition and our need for redemption. The redemptive work of Jesus Christ offers a pathway to restore our spiritual DNA, aligning it once again with God's original design. This transformation is beautifully captured in 2 Corinthians 5:17 (NIV):

"Therefore, if anyone is in Christ, the new creation has come: The old has gone, the new is here!"

Forensic Science and the Quest for Truth

The exploration of DNA in forensic science illustrated the pursuit of truth and justice, paralleling spiritual truths. Forensic science's meticulous analysis and the objective quest for facts resonate with the biblical call to seek and uphold truth. John 8:32 (NIV) declares:

"Then you will know the truth, and the truth will set you free."

The integration of forensic science into our understanding of God's DNA highlights the interconnectedness of physical and spiritual realms, demonstrating how scientific discoveries can enhance our spiritual understanding.

Ethical Considerations and the Sanctity of Life

Throughout our exploration, we encountered ethical considerations related to DNA and forensic science. Respecting the sanctity of life and the dignity of individuals aligns with the biblical principle of honoring the divine image in every person. Genesis 9:6 (NIV) emphasizes this:

"Whoever sheds human blood, by humans shall their blood be shed; for in the image of God has God made mankind."

These ethical considerations remind us of our responsibility to use scientific knowledge wisely and compassionately, ensuring that our actions reflect God's love and justice.

The Transformative Power of Spiritual DNA

Understanding our spiritual DNA underscores the transformative power of God's grace. Through faith in Christ, we experience a new birth, a renewal that aligns our lives with God's purpose. This transformation is ongoing, involving daily commitment and reliance on the Holy Spirit. Romans 12:2 (NIV) encourages us:

"Do not conform to the pattern of this world, but be transformed by the renewing of your mind. Then you will be able to test and approve what God's will is—his good, pleasing and perfect will."

Embracing Our Divine Heritage

As we embrace our identity as bearers of God's DNA, we are called to live out this reality in our daily lives. This involves reflecting on God's character, pursuing justice and truth, and nurturing our relationship with Him. Ephesians 4:22-24 (NIV) instructs:

"You were taught, with regard to your former way of life, to put off your old self, which is being corrupted by its deceitful desires; to be made new in the attitude of your minds; and to put on the new self, created to be like God in true righteousness and holiness."

Why Understanding God's DNA Is Important

Understanding God's DNA is crucial for several reasons:

1. Identity and Purpose: Recognizing that we are created in God's image provides a foundation for understanding our true identity and purpose. It affirms our worth and calls us to live in alignment with God's design.

2. Moral and Spiritual Guidance: God's DNA encompasses the moral and spiritual qualities we are called to embody. Understanding these qualities helps us navigate life's challenges with integrity and righteousness.

3. Redemption and Transformation: The concept of spiritual DNA highlights the transformative power of God's grace. Understanding our need for redemption and the process of spiritual renewal is essential for living a life that honors God.

4. Ethical Living: Understanding the sanctity of life and the divine image in every person guides our ethical decisions, ensuring that we act with compassion, justice, and respect for others.

5. Connection Between Science and Faith: Exploring the relationship between DNA and spirituality bridges the gap

between science and faith, enriching our understanding of both realms and demonstrating how they can complement each other.

Conclusion: A Call to Live Out God's DNA

As we conclude this exploration of God's DNA, let us commit to living out the divine blueprint imprinted within us. This involves daily surrender to God's will, pursuit of truth and justice, and reflecting His character in all we do. By embracing our identity as bearers of God's DNA, we honor our Creator and fulfill our purpose.

Philippians 1:6 (NIV) provides a fitting conclusion:

"Being confident of this, that he who began a good work in you will carry it on to completion until the day of Christ Jesus."

May we continue to grow in our understanding and application of God's DNA, living lives that glorify Him and draw others to His transformative love and truth.

SHIMBA
PUBLISHING

www.ingramcontent.com/pod-product-compliance
Lightning Source LLC
Chambersburg PA
CBHW061321120726
48001CB00002B/624
* 9 7 9 8 3 3 0 6 7 8 6 9 3 *